Wine From The Bottle

Table of Contents

1

It Runs In The Family

I grew up fearing rejection.
In turn, I grew up fearing my mother.

No matter how many years pass,
I still await a call that never comes.

Killer Instinct.

There is an instinct settled deep within me.
It grew from a millennia of waiting and a thousand more
sat wondering.
It grew with the ferocity of weeds cracking concrete, the
one plant that didn't need special care.

There is an instinct settled deep within me.
It was built out of necessity of survival.

There is an instinct rooted deep within, that screams for
me, pleads for me to leave before it's too late.

There is an instinct that chills me to the bone. One that
can slice even the thickest of bonds. One that calls upon
venom as naturally as a snake.

This is an instinct in which knives are embraced in white
knuckles and gritted teeth curl into smiles.

This is death in the acutest form.
A kind of murder that leaves no scene.
This is the death of a daughter who waited years for a
mother who never came.

As a child, I was rocket launched into space to achieve
success, to be the best.
now I find myself as nothing but an asteroid
 hurtling towards the cold abyss of outer space.

Jupiter, Saturn, Uranus, Neptune
I was told to succeed with no idea what that looks like.
Pluto is rapidly approaching, my joints are freezing.
Would it have been better to burn in the sun?

"Shoot for the moon and if you miss, you'll be among
the stars."

But the stars are scarce out here,
Oxygen levels are depleting,
The glass is cracking
Frost gathers on heavy eyelashes

I should have chosen to burn.

When did my youth expire?
When was it no longer acceptable to enjoy
"Childish" things?
At what age was I no longer your princess?
How did my youth pass me by
Before my twenty-first year?
Why did I start aging faster than my body did?

When I am dust and bones in a few years,
I will still ache for your attention.

Blue apples, green berries
Black lemons, wasp milkshakes
It's chaos, ma and chaos never ends.

My mind is spinning
Like spiders making their traps
The rain is pouring
Beating down on my body
As my feet pound on the ragged ground
It's chaos, Ma and chaos never ends.

I can feel my mind going.
I can't remember why I am here
Why am I running?
The tree is hard against my chest.
It's chaos, Ma and chaos never ends.

The forest floor is welcoming.
The wind howls like a sorrowful mother

Mother?

Mother, are you there?

                                Why aren't you answering?

Mother,

        I'm so cold.

They say the forgiving is for yourself
That the resentment you harbor only hurts you.

I don't want to forgive them
I'm not ready.
My hatred and resentment keeps me warm
I'm not ready to face the cold of its absence

If I hadn't been the eldest, I think I could've learned how to be. If there had been a daughter before me, maybe she would've shown me. Instead, my younger siblings got me. A halfway house for people with no intention of getting better. My incessant need to fix people.

If I hadn't been the eldest, if I hadn't been the example, I could have been human. I wouldn't relate to David Foster Wallace's "Everything I've ever let go of has claw marks". I could just be.

mostly, I hope your daughter never knows a man like him. I hope you see the warning signs of the boys interested in her as a direct mirror of your best friend. How they guilt and berate and persuade to achieve what they want.

I have searched for your love in every corner of my past and found closed doors.

Raised between "never loving enough" and "keeping love just out of reach", I am ravenous.

I finish men the way a recovering addict finishes packs of gum, quickly, mindlessly. Unwrap, chew, spit. Unwrap, chew, spit. The monotony consumes me, all of them exactly the same. *Maneater maneater maneater.* Consume or <u>be</u> consumed.

Devour

Whenever a man shows interest in me, a feeling awakens within me. It is not sexual in nature, but it is relentless and hungry.

A man is to be devoured and not to be trusted with sensitive matters.

A man is to be devoured before he gets the jump on you.

Heed my warning, eat their heart first before substantial damage occurs to yours.

Plagued, am I with the self-awareness to realize how similar I truly am to each of my parents. Traits they hated about each other, the most glaringly obvious within me. It's an odd thing to know you're so similar to the other parent while one talks bad about the other.

"God, she's so-"

"He's such a-"

"So am I. So am I!"

I wanted to scream at them as a child. I am all of those things and more. My parents' harsh words against each other turn inwards in me. All of those things that were bad in the other, must also be bad in me.

My mother calling me her "mini me" and my father calling her a "bitch". Does that not also extend to me? My mother calling my father a "Jackass" for something I also do. Does that not extend to me?

Where do my parents stop and I begin? It's a maddening way of thinking. A railway with no end. You can't get off the train once you get on. Stations full of people and I am alone on a bullet train speeding past. "I am more than them" I want to call out to them, "I'm more than them, I'm better than them".

A keen eye for details and micro expressions, the commuters blink at my plight.

As a child, I always hated the silence.

Adored the quiet but hated the silence.

There was something so unnerving about a silent room.

The way my ears would begin to buzz along with the lightbulb above.

A quiet room is calm. A quiet room has people doing their own thing.

A silent room is a waiting game.

I will face death as it crudely knocks at my door,
I will face the harshness of the world
Take in the pain of the world around me before I am
ever able
To face you without that all too familiar tug in my chest
and match strike under my eyes.

Lost

Once, you ran with the Lost Boys of Neverland,
Now, you curse the nights that never end.
You curse the winters and their biting cold.
You curse me and my bloody hands,
Sliced on the glass of who you once were.
You curse anyone who tries to help you,
Then wonder why you feel so alone.
        And when you grow old without a hand to hold,
                        The blame will be someone else's

Impiety is a suffocating concept.

How can one be impious,
If they, themselves, are God?
Nothing but subjects under them,
Ready to bend to their will.
Believe in them. Praise them. Praise me.
Out there, on that wooden stage,
I am their god.
Their applause is more addicting
Than any drug out there.
Jumped through hoops, tore myself apart mentally, bled
to feel that rush.
From the first hit, I couldn't give it up.
Mother always said one hit was all it took.
But she never mentioned this.
Never mentioned the very voices
Hitting back at the platform
Would be my overdose.
My fall from grace.
Oh, how merciless,
How impious they were.

Tales from the lemon grove, pt. 1

Nature has no concept of good or bad.
The rains give way to life
And take it away.
When the harsh winters melt away
The leaves return
Adding color back to
The lifeless terrains.
My youth seemed to fly by,
What is my purpose in life?
Do I serve others?
Or shall I wither in my mother's arms, Unseen.
My siblings have gone out
Made others happy
Served their purpose.
I've been stuck here
In mother's arms for so long
My skin is aging
Wilting.
I'll be useless soon.
My body will feed the ground.
Nature returning to nature.

Tales From the Lemon Grove, pt. 2

Bitter and bruised,
I'm still looking for a way out of the lemon grove, for a way out of being my mother's daughter.

September beckons and the grove tightens around the contents of my chest cavity. We may never escape what is engraved in our bones, what is written deep within our DNA. I may never escape this lemon grove, may never escape my fate of a lemon which never falls from the branch.

Hometowns and fields of flowers
Hide horrific secrets of young buds
Picked too soon.
In beauty and comfort
nobody wants to leave,
their hearts tied down.
Love is a war
Hearts broke, bloody hands
Going home to hugs
Greeted with a kiss from a lover like a soldier.
Waking up from the illusion.
Lie to me. Say the war is justified.
The victory was worth the pain.
When the party's over and you're picking up petals
Do you think of me and our once beautiful lie?
"All's fair in love and war" and yet this doesn't seem fair.

Innocence gets tangled in a rose bush
Their thorns pricking a child's hand,
who was distracted by their beauty.

Sitting in your parent's house,
The lie still lingers like flowers in a vase.
Bore

I bore the shame of hundreds of women who came before me, who craved more than this. I once traced my maternal line to five hundred some AD, a large portion of them dying before the age of forty, all mothers to a large brood of children. I wonder what their hopes and ambitions were and feel guilty as I try to see them as human, just as I struggle to see my mother as such. A tightness in my throat, a strangulation of expectation- my grandmother was a writer too in her youth. Married away at just fifteen to a man in his twenties. My aunt never had children and I find myself selfishly wondering if she was the lucky one in all of this. A grandmother several hundred years back, name lost to history, killed by her husband at twenty-four, poisoned, so that he may remarry. No date of birth, no history of existing outside of her death. Centuries between us and yet, no matter how much I search for it, I don't even know her name- no way of keeping her alive.

Mothers and daughters into mothers leading to me. I wonder if this shame is generational or carved into womanhood. A metallic iron taste from thousands of years of biting their tongues. Born with it, I think. A shame mothers feel being unable to save their daughters from the same fate. But I've got my father's scarred hands, hands that have slipped down the handle

of the knife I've used to kill and recreate myself
thousands of times over again. I don't know how to stop
feeling guilty. I'm closer to thirty than I am the girl who
could love her mother freely and saw her as bigger than
the whole world. She cries in my chest; I don't know
how to get her to stop. I've smothered her hundreds of
times, her blood on my hands, under my nails, I can't get
clean. I don't know how to stop feeling guilty. I bear her
in my hips as my mother once did at twenty. Let me
rebirth you, I think. I'll protect you better this time. I'll
be better and see the signs. I'll wear my glasses as my
mother did but to you, I won't be blind. I'll cradle you
close to my chest.

Mothers to daughters into mothers.
I'll be overbearing if it meant saving you from the
flowers that take root in your lungs, saving you from the
metallic taste on your tongue. Saving you from men who
are bores who call women whores. Let me rebirth you,
I'll do right by you. I'll help you over the sidewalk so you
may not silently slip through the cracks. I don't know
how to stop feeling guilty. My own mother's absence
bore through me like a hammer to drywall, patched but
the hole remains. I don't know how to stop feeling
guilty.

Drunken Atonement (Set Me Free)

I thought you'd linger like a ghost after you left,
They said you would-
But you didn't.
In the darkest of days,
In the coldest of summers,
You're gone.
You're just gone.
No note. No phone call.
Just silence.
Mind numbing silence.
Mind numbing cold.

It's different.
You get used to death but never this,
The abruptness, the lack of reason.
This never-ending night, a sleep I cannot wake up from.
Who am I without you?

-when you left you took all the
warmth of the world with you

A sound clicks and the movie starts
In crowds, I look for you
But you seem to always find me first.
For a moment, I am not me
And it seems like,
Just for a moment, we could be

We move in sync,
You cannot say that you don't care for me,
Like I care for you
Because lying is a sin.
But it's as they say
Nobody cares until you're dead.

You're dead.
There's nothing I can say,
Nothing I can do,
That could bring you back.

To bring you back would take an act of God,
And we were nothing if not sinners.

In the back row
sits a girl, a ghost of you
fitting, I suppose, for a class
studying the past.
whenever I see her
I only see you and all my mistakes.
It's almost cathartic.
The girl has no bad memory of me.
We've only spoken once so she's luckier than most.

I watched as you aged,
Now I know not what you did yesterday.
A sister that was never mine to have- though a sister
nevertheless.
We buried each other in words never to be said
Killed each other in the flames of our actions

The thing about loss is that it lingers.
In not so obvious ways.
I have never been afraid of death.
It's natural.
 I've seen a lot of loved ones go.

No, the hard thing about death
is what comes after someone's gone.

Those of you who live,
Who survived are left yearning.

A crater in your life only they can fill
You still look for them during the holidays
And in shopping aisles

They say grief is love with
No home to return to.
But how could they possibly understand
That my only home, was you?

I wish I stayed as mean as I thought I was in elementary school,
I wish my nails never grew into the talons they have become.

There are a thousand wishes in my heart,
a thousand brewed cups of tea left standing, forgotten.

I've grown from the angry child left in the stairwells of my heart,
forgiven myself for the damage I have caused others,

and yet, I cannot bring it within myself to forgive what I did to you.
I look at you, a ghost of the friend that I loved so dearly and destroyed in a single night, and I can't do it.

I would not forgive me either.

I wish I knew the last time I saw you would have been the last time ever. Maybe I would have cherished our time together even more, taking my time to engrave you into the core of my being.

I loved you from the moment I laid my six-year-old eyes on you. It's the kind of love that lasts eternity and then some. I have nowhere to put all this love for you. It's wave after wave of grief that I can't fully comprehend.

We never got the chance to say goodbye. No tearful embrace, no memory of you in pain. In my mind, a thousand what ifs run amok. What if I hadn't gone to bed early that summer night, what if I had had my ringer on. Would you have been happy to see me in your final moments like you had been for any of our other visits?

Now everything I have left of you is contained in a cherry wood urn.

My personal Judas

The closest bonds become the thickest chains. My judge, my jury, and regrettably, my executioner, my very own Judas.
The wood of the bridge that could have been a life raft, was the same wood used to drown me.

You cast the first stone and blamed me for your wrongdoings.

You chopped the tree that became my crucifix and watched as they threw their stones.

When the end of the world came and life ceased to continue, I was perplexed to find that life Had gone on and was actively passing me by. How could this be? Did nobody know that life as we- as I knew it, had ended? That a higher power had given me the option to evolve quickly or die out. Change or die. You cannot continue as you are right now. I changed everything about me to survive and everybody I knew stayed the same. I outgrew everyone I loved and desperately tried to hold onto them as if I were still the one, they thought me to be.

It's New Years,

I'm shaking from the buzz in the air
But there's something else lingering.
TEN, NINE, EIGHT
Something more sinister.
The turning of the clock meets the turning of a new leaf
SEVEN, SIX, FIVE
The wine in my glass serves many a purpose
But mostly?
FOUR, THREE, TWO
It's just relief
ONE. HAPPY NEW YEAR!
Another year gone
I'll never have to be 16 again.

If the world was ending,

Where would you go?
Where would you run?
What would your first thought be
If you heard gunshots downstairs?
Constantly aware
Constantly vigilant
Never relaxing because
You are always prepared for the worst.

What's the worst that could happen?
It's just one drink
One drink at a party is all it takes.
What will the future bring?
When will this charade end,
When will the mask be removed,
When will you see me?
The future, should it ever arrive,
Is suggestive to change.
But life is cruel.
So when the world ends,
Where would you like to be?

When God casts His final judgment,
whom will He be judging:
 me or the monster of my flesh?

Is there a separation?
Am I as tainted as my flesh?
How deep does the filth and uncleanliness run?

How could I ever be worthy with hands like these?

I often felt as if I needed proof of residence of my own
body, proof of ownership.
Proof,
That's what you wanted, right?
He said, she said,
It was my word against his,
And you were never going to listen to mine
You can't play both sides.
In this Game, there are no winners or losers.
No starting lines,
No stadium lights with a marching band playing,
And no proof of ownership.
There aren't pictures of handprints or bruises,
The wounds this game inflicts aren't visible to the naked
eye.
When they found my body, You said nothing.
Autopsy read abuse
And yet you saw no use
in believing it. Or maybe you did,
and you felt too much loyalty
To a man good enough to be dickhead royalty.

Melancholic Spirits

I crave human intimacy so much

I will flay myself to the bone

Expose my nerves to the world like I'm not afraid of the pain that will come with it.

I will expose every little thought that pops in my head, every joke I can muster.

Please look but don't touch.

Learn everything and absolutely nothing about me.

See: the dirt on my face and the broken epitaph at my feet,

See: my lips and the white lies they tell.

Look at me. Oh god I'm begging you, please look at me.

Eyes are on me, eyes that look but don't see.

Ears that hear but don't listen.

I can be your Starry Night Over the Rhône, painted pretty for the whole world to see. I can be your Houdini, your escapist, so long as you don't hold séances in my wake.

When tomorrow comes, I will try once more to tear myself apart for you.

"Where are you hurt?"

My eyes burn in tears that cannot shed,

Lips that dare not mutter a tangible thought.

The cat is scratching the bag, having already feasted on my tongue.

It's three in the morning.

My throat is sore from the rapid beating of my heart.

Chest is tight from the words that won't leave.

I'm trying to tell you, but I can't open my mouth.

Everywhere.

It's 4 am.

The night owls have gone to bed and the witches have long since retired.

It's 4 am and all I can think of is you. I'm selfish in my thoughts. I take ownership of things that are not my burden and obsess over mistakes I have made.

It's 4 am and you're an eternal golden hour, adored by everyone. I regret the days I spent glaring at the sun. I never appreciated you for what you were.

It's 4 am and the wet on my cheeks rivals the morning's dew.

It's 4 am and it's been months since I've slept alone. Bleary eyes shine in the blue light. The lack of sleep is nothing in comparison to the loneliness and pain I feel tonight.

I suppose this makes you right.

Fight or flight finally set in and I chose spite.

You loved me because I was fun
I was adventurous , I was high on life
I was impulsive and you liked that because
We got along so well.

When the night turned and
the wine poured a little quicker
And the girl you loved slipped into a ghostly shell,
I was no longer fun.
I was cold. I was tired all the time,
I was miserable, a fake, a fraud
And you just didn't know how you didn't see it coming.

When the sun rises, that girl will return
With a wild look in her eyes and a taste
For adventure, swearing that this time she's better
This time, she's there to stay.

                    -vicious cycles and a glint of mania

Shall I be cursed to tear myself open for
as long as I can blink, and cry, and write?
Cursed to use my blood and tears as ink
in my dancing pen? Are my shattered bones enough?
Is my heart broken to your liking?
When all my aching and suffering is exhausted,
Shall I repeat myself like a broken record
Or succumb to my eternal anguish?
When the ink has run dry and I am but
A discarded sonnet on a mad poet's floor
Who will know of it?

I shall go mad in the name of creation

My poems are too literary and the several drafts of books in my computer- too poetic. The wires in my brain for each of them, intertwined and between it all, is me. I cannot separate myself from my writings and musings.

I cannot separate myself from the sickly sadness that infects everything I touch. They always seem embedded with a sadness I cannot shake. A desperation that clings to every word begging anyone to free them from the prison I have constructed.

I fear that, like my poetry and literature, my sadness and I are one and the same.

Someday, Somedays

Somedays, the melancholy won't leave me. It sits in this desolate waiting room a few seats down. Staring at me with unseeing eyes, or rather all seeing- which is worse, I'm not sure.

I think it will always be like this, somedays. I stare out at the sunrise, and billions of people over the course of human history stare back. It's the same sun, I'm sitting with the same familiar stranger in the waiting room. I'm the same bits of matter as people born and gone millions of years before me.

Somedays, the tears fall all too easily during the night and when the sun rises, the waiting room won't be as barren.

When they lowered my coffin,
I was still screaming.
Carved chasms in the cheap plywood
Only serve to remind me that
                    No one is coming

No knight in shining armor,
No helpless friend,
No one.
No one is coming to save me from this hell,
From myself.

Dried red fingertips transition from splinters to cold
earth.
When I reach the top,
Will anyone recognize me beyond this shell of a person?

I feel like life is passing me by,
I'm sixteen alone at an underwater
Movie theater watching a poorly made
Coming-of-age indie film.
I often feel as stable as nitroglycerin left unattended.
My mind is a playground- if the playground
Was a minefield with hundreds of bouncing balls.
You try your best to pretend that I am fine,
that I am getting better, but I'm not.
Most days it feels like it will never get better.
14 years and it still hasn't felt like
Everything will be okay
No glimmer of hope
Not matter how many times
I am reassured that I'll be fine
My mind races, googling my symptoms

Google search: how long is a lifetime with bipolar?
Google search: Why am I a mean friend?
Google search: (random actor) height
Google search: how many microorganisms in my body
aren't mine?
Google search: how to lose weight fast

When the moon rises and everyone is fast asleep,
I'll curl up and hit rewind.

You wished you could say your depression was like Santa Claus, only coming around once a year- but it wasn't just a wintertime affair, was it? It settled firmly like concrete sometime early 2008. As a kid, you were always lonely. Alone and under-stimulated, the young brain sees shadows that aren't there, whispers and laughter carrying in from empty rooms, voices that carry harsh tones, and an intense desire to escape.

You know exactly why you are the way that you are, but self-awareness makes it worse.

Growing up, your friends had exactly what you wanted. Attentive parents, siblings that didn't bully and berate, a family that never forgot birthdays or walked out of school performances early. They were thin and their heads weren't too big. You were envious and your jealousy turned inwardly venomous. At nine years old, you decided you hated yourself. Becoming a grandmaster of emotional chess won't make the loneliness go away. I wish I could have told you that, but hindsight is 20/20.

I can't sleep at night when dating someone new.
Terrified to wake up and realize it has started anew.
That, despite my best wishes and careful pickings,
Every man will be exactly like you.

Everywhere I look, the people know.
what it's like to love and to be loved
To feel safe and comfortable in another's arms
A manual must have been handed out in the teenage
years that teaches you how
I must have missed class that day.
I look upon my friends and feel left out
I've done my part, I've *played* the part
But a performance only lasts so long.
I'm full of a thousand wishes.
I wish I didn't feel the need to pretend.
I wish I didn't hurt the ones I care about
I wish I had done things differently.
I wish the show would have ended differently.

I wish I could love someone.
I wish there was someone worthy of it.
I can pretend like I'm above it, but I'm not.
At the end of the day, I'm just a girl
Cold and alone in a big world filled with lovers.

To Sam,

There are days where I am happy and enjoying life. Other days I am mourning the girl you could've become if you had been given the chance. They say what doesn't kill you makes you stronger, but you didn't need to be strong. You were just a kid. You needed to be protected and I'm sorry they couldn't do that. I'm sorry I couldn't protect you. I can see your eight-year-old eyes staring at me in the eyes of my cousins. I see them in broken promises and fingers crossed behind backs. I see them in hospital paperwork wondering who I've become. I see them in my dreams of having children of my own. I see your innocent blue eyes in feelings of loneliness, much too young to know what that felt like. I see you when I bend who I am to please others. And when you felt like the weight of the world was on your sixteen-year-old shoulders, no matter how grown I thought you were, I remember that I was just a kid. A kid much too young to be exposed to the world of loneliness.

The smell of sweets fills the air- full of laughter and
happy times.
My heartbeat is rising now.
They're expecting me back any moment now.
Gleaming lights of gold dance in eyes made of glass
Quivering bows drawn,
Arrows will strike any minute.
Food is a prison and Laughter the unfortunate jailer.
Heart Rate is in the hundreds now as chatter seems to
increase with it.
The beats a tempo and they are an orchestra,
Orchestrating a holiday gathering as
                    imprisoning as this one.
Brief pauses in the conversation and I wince.
I've been gone too long.
Oh, they won't be happy.

Maybe I imagine things.

"Your labs came back fine."
What. How can that be possible? Why can't you see that I'm ill?
I'm sick. I'm sick. I'm Sick I'm Sick I'm Sick I'm Sick Im Sick
Can you not hear the frantic beat of my heart?
Can you not see how easily my skin bruises?
Can't you hear the crackling of my young knees?
Can you not see the cold sweat and how it glistens on my body?
"How much do you weigh?"
Why aren't you listening to me?
I AM SICK.
I'm sick. I'm sick. I'm sick I'm sick I'm sick I'm sick I'm sick
I find myself wishing I had a serious illness so that you would finally listen,
So that my pain would be validated.
"When was the date of your last menstrual period?"
three years ago.
A twenty-one-year-old, who has had under forty periods in her entire life, has gone three years without one and is complaining of pain. Don't you see the issue in that?

My body is falling apart and you're asking if I'm sexually active.

Why can't you understand that something is wrong?

-just a woman seeking medical care

51

They say that hate is the opposite of love,
But that is simply not true.
The opposite of hate and love is indifference.
It has taken me eons to feel indifferent towards you,
I let your actions influence mine
And yet, your words continue to linger in my mind

Mindful of the cracks in the sidewalk,
I walked carefully hand in hand with you,
But that was before
Before it started

It's over now.
My life is free from yours and yet...
Yet, I still find myself troubled.
Troubled by your words, your cruel words,
And even crueler actions.
Those actions continue to plague me
four years afterwards.
What consumed so much of my mind,
barely scratches yours.
Throughout my life I believed myself cursed.
Cursed to carry the burden of everyone's faults and
mistakes.

Cursed to never know my chest without that crushing weight, my very own Maleficent, cursing me in my cradle. Punishing me for existing

You call me Sunshine and yet,
I am cursed to live only the darkest nights.
You are what you love and if that makes me a rose made of nectarine,
It almost makes me sad to see it withering.

If I am sunshine shining two decades long
Then I was set up to fail.
I was set up to burn everyone I meet.

If I am sunshine, I hurt the ones who love me. I'll leave you dehydrated, the kind where it feels like cotton in your mouth and dries out your crops.
I'm too much for some people. The ones who prefer the cold, who have a heat intolerance. The ones living in an eternal winter.
I am too much all the time, getting worse every summer.
Record high heats and droughts on the west coast.
I cut winters short and dominate autumn,
One day the sun will consume the universe and I will be left with no one to burn.

Metal casings hitting linoleum, sulfur and rust filling the air, a ruler on the ground and a pair of scissors next to him, another front-page headline.

And so, I'll keep you in my thoughts and my prayers, never actually doing something to keep you safe. I have the ability to do so, I think, as they lower yet another of your friends, siblings, children. But oh, how money talks so you'll remain the topic of Congress floor mocks.

You stand there with your businesses and side-hustles as if any of it truly matters. You make your inventions and charge whatever set price you want in this unregulated economy, for fun. I had my business ventures in the past, but I've been through literal hell since. I stared God in the face and guess what, the sky was empty.

I do some of my best thinking alone- in the dead of night, in the earliest hours of morning, lights off in the shower, long since running cold. I am trying to think my way out of myself and this hellish minefield I have created. I am trying to think of ways to bring you home- of ways I could have brought you back home if I had not been so small and how I just might have been the reason you didn't come back.

The cold water turns lukewarm on my face as I imagine what it would be like if you did come back. Would you show up in person for me for the first time ever or would it be a message through whatever relevant social media that took seconds to fire off? Would I even care if you did? Years down the line since your absence, I hardly even notice the massive aching hole punched through my chest.

The water flows in and out of it, the edges, one long hypertrophic scar, inflamed from my own hands reaching in and pulling bits of myself out for other people- in hopes they will not leave me too. Pulling the last bits of domesticity from my chest, a feral creature slowly replaces me. Will it even matter how much I give of myself to others if I no longer resemble the one who gave me away?

Last Call (Call Me A Cab)

Potential lovers are placed on impossibly high pedestals,
She doesn't blink when they fall from it.
Brash, cold, and rough on all edges.
They are hurt in the name of obtaining love from a
woman who will die alone.
Old and decrepit, an unruly spinstress.

Day after day, she watches as life passes.
She will never be able to recognize a winner if she saw
one,
forever sabotaging their love life.
A painful memory,
the girl who threw them away
 like it was nothing more than a stain on her ledger.

The woman who made their lives a game.

Myth

I'm sick of poetry about Icarus and Odysseus, of Ophelia going mad and of Lady MacBeth puppeteering her husband. I'm sick of the Gods and the Myths and the religions. I'm sick of the half-truths and alluding to an everyday, casual love to allusions. Icarus died and so will your love.

Going, going, gone.

We always knew it would end like this.

My attachment danced on a tightrope for months,

Yours, two feet firmly on the ground.

I always knew I had weak ankles,

I had horrible balance as a kid.

But on the tightrope,

Miles in the air,

Eyes dancing on me like a petting zoo animal,

The foundation is steady and you're on your knee,

Get up or I'll fall from this tightrope.

Get off your knee, lest I fall from your favor

Do you know?

Know that the stars, the very object of beauty in the sky,

are formed in your eyes

Eyes that know mine

Better than I know mine.

Do you know that when you look at him,

I'm screaming inside?

Did you know

Know that you held my heart

My fragile heart in your hands

Did you know

Know that I would have dropped everything

And anyone to fix you?

But you don't, so I won't.

I won't, so you don't.

We keep going on and on

And on and on and on and on...

In circles,

A continuous game of cat and mouse,

A single moment frozen in time.

In thousands of years when they find us encased in ice,

Will archeologists know the life we left behind?

Will historians know that I froze for you?

Will the poets argue over our tragedy?

There are days where I cannot drag myself out of bed, much preferring to just sink into the foam and springs, rotting away until nothing remains. Sometimes the days are far and few between, other times they come more often than not.

Constant stimulation as to not allow my brain even one second to cut me down. The only thing I have, the only comfort is knowing that life goes on. While I might rot away, the sun will still rise, the clouds will still bring about rain. People all around the globe are having better days, and I want to join them.

They say I will have this illness forever, that it will never leave and I will spend the rest of my life having to manage it by worshipping pill bottles and cognitive behavioral therapy. This is how I will always be. It's a vicious cycle. I regain a sense of normalcy and it slips away like water in my hands. They say it likely came from somewhere in my family tree, sneaking up behind me and digging its claws in. I get in my own way, and still the sun will rise.

The stars carved themselves
Onto my arm when I was only a child,
Leaving the Big Dipper in its wake.
They say stars shine their brightest
Right before they collapse
And my darling,
I can't breathe, I can't sleep.
Is this my collapse?

No, I have already collapsed,
This is my rebirth.
Like the stars,
I, too, am an exposed ball of energy.
You're like the stars too,
From what I've seen.
Lonely in the great abyss
Yet, surrounded by peers.

I am merely a child looking
 to the North Star to guide me home.
Will you walk with me, just for tonight?

I want to live on after I am gone.

I'm terrified of being forgotten.

Immortalize me in your words- even if they are bad ones.

For once, I want to be loved.

For once, I want to be someone's muse.

You don't have to be so angry with the world, don't have to be so angry with other people. It isn't their fault they aren't like you. They don't see things the same way as you do, you can't change that. It's okay if you can't always see the bigger picture, if some days you only see in hues of blue, brown, and red. That's okay, because you're you.

If I could fall in love, I'd want it to be with you.

For someone who lives in black and white,
The gray we made became my addiction.
I'll spend my whole life getting over it.

It Lingers

You've yet to ask, and it lingers between us like a guest overstaying their welcome.

I've yet to say anything, my silence has never been louder, my clothed body has never been more exposed.

It weighs on my chest, a confession that has fallen from my lips before, never honest until now

You've never looked more inviting, and yet I've never been more scared of my shadow.

Shake the feeling.

Try as I might,
I cannot shake the feeling that I was crafted for love.
I was not born of it but oh, I was made for it.

It's all I crave. I was made to love someone- completely,
obsessively.
I'd like to believe I could love someone- softly, quietly.
-as if loving someone would take the heaviness from my
step and the indifference off my tongue
-as if devoting myself to a true and honest love would, in
turn, make a true and honest woman of me.

I hope you never hurt yourself for the way you learned to cope and survive.
Be gentle with yourself,
It wasn't your fault they never loved you the way you needed to be loved.
It wasn't your fault you were born with the wrong body.

What exactly makes yogurt Greek?

I consume so much, it courses through my veins.
I know it will hurt me but I do it anyway.
The only thing my body accepts and equally rejects.
My intestines curl,
my stomach turns at what makes my brain happy.
What I enjoy so much hurts.
The things I love will always destroy me.

I think I fall in love a little with every person I meet.
Not in a romantic sense, I absolutely adore them.
I adore people. I adore them in their purest form.
How they behave when no one is watching,
how they interact with others,
the excitement on their faces when they see animals.

I think I often fall in love with what people could be.

Christmas Ales (Take Me Home)

Petrichor

Noun: a pleasant smell that frequently accompanies the first rain after a long period of warm, dry weather.

A warm earthy smell. A comforting warmth reminiscent of sleepily pulling your lover closer in the early hours of the morning as the birds chirp. In those moments when life is slowed down, when there is no demand for your time, gone is the storm and the smell of petrichor settles in with the morning dew.

A new beginning.

Numbered Days

I hope to find you,

The one so perfectly made for me, and I so perfectly made for them,

I hope to find you so that our souls may meet once more.

I hope to find you, the one person who may understand some better than anyone else ever has. That you find me in the piles of other sonnets laid at my feet of lovers that didn't stick and understand the crinkles in my paper and choose to love me regardless.

I hope you find me because our days on this planet are numbered, and I don't want to spend an eternity knowing true love passed me by.

When you find me, judge me not by my rough exterior but the contents of my heart. Because loving you makes me a better person, because loving you is the sweet smell of petrichor.

Love

For as long as I shall live,
the words "I love you" shall never fall from my lips.
Afterall, they're just words.
How could three little words possibly convey my
thoughts,
how could three words spoken
trillions of times over the course of human history
satiate me.

I would rip the lungs from my chest,
And present them as a macabre bouquet,
That would mean more than those words.

Take my beating heart and do with it as you please,
It's always been yours,
 I cannot spend another moment
pretending as if there could possibly be anyone else for
me.

I used to pity Icarus and his hubristic ways. Longing so much to fly, he flew too close to the sun in defiance of the gods and burned. Death by fire is not an ideal way to go.
I could never imagine longing for something so much you'd be willing to die for just an ounce of freedom that Icarus had felt. Your eyes met mine in a crowded room
and I understood.
Eyes so dark and rich, I wanted so desperately to know what secrets they held.
Your smile, good god, your smile.
You had a smile so divine, it lit up the room.

Is it painful to be that gorgeous?

To stand in a room knowing everyone would kill just to talk to you?
How cruel your smile is. It taunts me. Beckons me closer. Face to Face and I can't breathe.
I want to trace the details of your skin, every scar and freckle, engraving them in my mind.
Your eyes have the slightest specks of honey brown that set my soul ablaze.
I pitied Icarus until I understood him.
I'd burn for your love,
I'd burn for your praise,
I'd burn for you.

There are a few things he is in this life

Like he is the ground beneath my feet and the jacket holding my arms in a hugging manner. He is a quiet lullaby lulling me into a dreamless sleep on a starless night.

He is a ghost and I, his mourning widow. He is the morning air and I have been deprived of oxygen for years.

He is pain, but so am I. Our pain is so inexhaustibly intertwined, like a pair of hedgehogs huddling for warmth. To be human is to love without restraint and with the acceptance of the human condition.

"Love me"

The words burn as they rip from my throat.

Love me. See me. Silence.

"Love me" he begs and my gut churns. Silence.

I have no previous love to compare this to.

Only tv shows and tear stained copies of Jane Austen and scratched CD copies of an artist echoing my youth to compare this to.

Dozens of stage lights burned my retinas from years of playing pretend could never have prepared me for this.

You were the love that came without warning. You're the first person I want to tell when something exciting happens or the only one who can comfort me when I'm upset.

The only love I'm truly terrified of losing. I'm terrified of losing you, because one day you will wake up and realize that I was only as good as you made me. Just like everyone else did. Please don't let me tear us apart. Don't let me ruin the only love I've ever known.

I always dreamed of a truly profound love- not unlike that of poets passed. A magnificent ideal that an ordinary person could experience a love that could move mountains. A secret hopeless romantic all my life, I just thought I wasn't worthy of something like that, so I scoffed at the idea. Rolled my eyes at couples and informed my friends that statistically their high school boyfriends would break up with them and that they weren't actually soulmates. I became a pessimist so others could never see how much I truly craved love. I acted above it and the boys and men who chased my affections- never to fully receive it. I hated that I had never romantically loved someone. I was damaged goods and made everyone around me look at the dumpster.

Nowadays, I'm not such a pessimist, though not exactly an optimist. I dream not of a profound love, but a quiet, soft love. A Sunday morning kind of love. Simplistic dates and a partner who truly sees me. A picnic by the river, under a tree. The spring flowers are in full bloom, there's a nice breeze. It's simple and romantic and personal. My poems about past hurts and how they still haunt me like a ghost would turn into poetry about how the wind blows through their hair or how a bird swept in and stole my sandwich or how they laughed until they were red in the face. I'd love them the way I love my friends and family- quietly and without much fuss.

Take a seat, child.

You are not Atlas; you do not have to carry the weight of the world on your shoulders. You owe them nothing. Not a smile, not your kindness, nothing.

Take a seat.

You are not the mythic chosen one, fated and prophesied to save everyone from destroying themselves. It would be unfair to even consider asking a child like you.

Take a seat and breathe.

You are not a world leader with nuclear launch codes and a short temper. You may never severely impact the world but then again, it is not your job to do so.

Breathe slowly, in and out.

Go play outside. Feel the wind blow through your hair and the blades of grass under your bare feet. Make potions of mud and grass and sticks. The mud is caking under your nails and the crevices of your knuckles and around the cup of water you smuggled from the kitchen.

Breathe and live free, my child.

One day, I won't write anymore. The words will no longer stir in my stomach and vomit onto any empty page or word document. I will have said everything that I need to say, exhausted every twisted outlet of my pain until it shriveled up and decaying.

Finding no use in beating a dead horse, I will write my final words and perhaps not even realize they are my last. The stories and verses racing in my mind as I try to sleep, itching to get out, will stop running and my mind will be quiet after all these years. I was a very sad and lonely kid, using reading and writing as an escape, but one day I won't need to escape. My breath and being won't reek of word vomit and blood that I used as ink in my pen. Will further words be hollow and vacant without the infusion of my suffering?
 I often wonder if my favorite poets and authors felt the same way as I do, the never-ending melancholy and need to get the words out before they drown in them. I feel so connected and disconnected from them. The melancholy became too much for some of them, but I'm determined to beat this. I think of writing as a lifeboat in a raging ocean, I'm lying on my back staring up at the midnight sky- cloudy, raining, waiting for the lights of the coast guard.

www.ingramcontent.com/pod-product-compliance
Lightning Source LLC
Chambersburg PA
CBHW021138020426
42331CB00005B/822